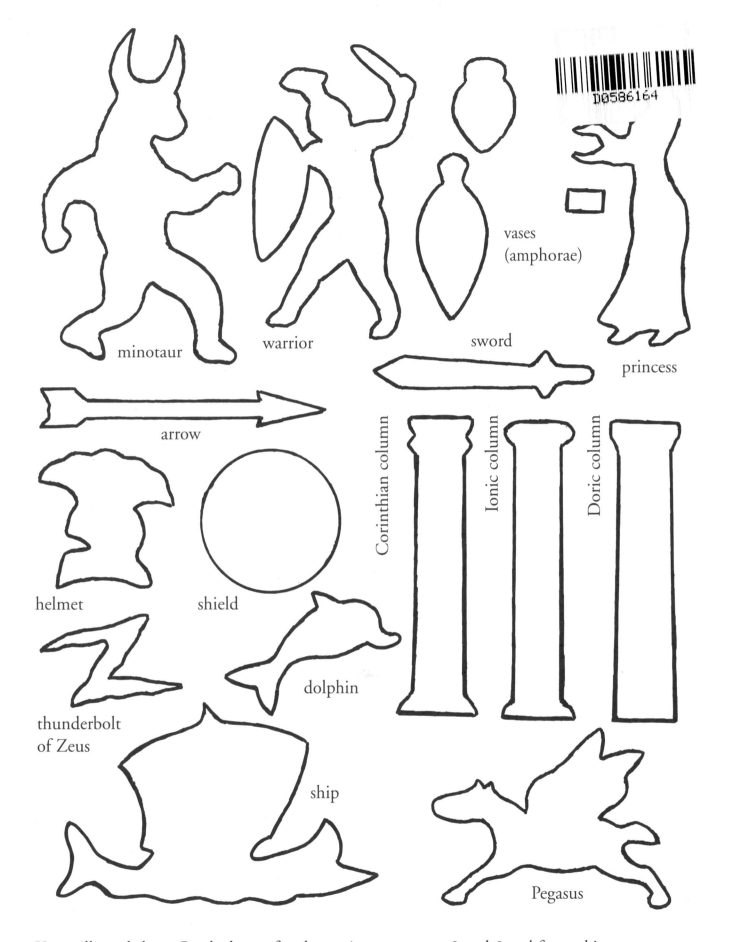

minotaur

warrior

vases
(amphorae)

sword

princess

arrow

Corinthian column

Ionic column

Doric column

helmet

shield

dolphin

thunderbolt
of Zeus

ship

Pegasus

You will need these Greek shapes for the projects on pages 2 and 8 and for making up your own myths. See opposite for how to use them. These instructions replace the ones on page 24.

# CONTENTS

Whatever you choose to make first you'll need plenty of packaging, so it's a good idea to start collecting it in advance. Ask people to save things for you instead of throwing them away.

You can flatten cardboard boxes and cereal packets to save space. Rinse plastic bottles and leave them to dry. Prepare an area to work in and have lots of old newspapers handy if you are using glue and paints.

# HOW TO MAKE A MAGIC BRACELET

Amphitrite was the wife of the sea god, Poseidon, and queen of the seas. Dolphins helped him to win her heart by speaking softly to her of his love. There were many dolphins living in the Mediterranean then. In the Greek myths, they guided ships and took messages for Poseidon.

He loves you.

Yeah, yeah, yeah!

**YOU'LL NEED:**
A clean plastic pot, sandpaper, scissors, acrylic paint and brushes, gold and silver pens, PVA glue, plaster filler and stencil.

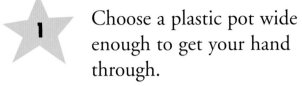

**1** Choose a plastic pot wide enough to get your hand through.

**2** Carefully cut off the bottom. Watch out for sharp edges!

**3** Roughen the outer surface with the sandpaper and paint with white acrylic paint.

**4** Decorate using the dolphin stencil, gold and silver pens and paint.

**5** You could mix a very small amount of plaster filler and PVA with the paint to make the dolphins stand out.

### TOP TIP – TOP TIP
When it's dry, paint all over with undiluted PVA glue. This will protect it and keep the colours bright.

**6** Leave a space to write your name using the Greek letters on pages 10-11.

# HOW TO MAKE A MEDUSA HEAD SHIELD

Meet Medusa the Gorgon. Just one look will turn you to stone but, by looking at her only in the reflection on his highly polished shield, Perseus was able to cut off her head. Perseus gave the head to the goddess Athene. She put it on the front of her shield.

Thanks, just what I always wanted.

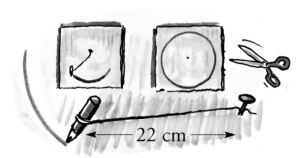

**1** Glue the pieces of cardboard together with the corrugations going in opposite ways.

**2** Draw a circle 44 cm in diameter on the cardboard. Use a pencil tied to the nail. Then cut it out.

**3** Make 2 small holes about 10 cm apart near the centre of the shield.

**4** Cut 2 eye shapes from the tub lid. Make a small hole in each.

Front                    Back

**5** Glue these over the holes in the shield.

**6** Thread the string through the eye holes. Leave a loop at the back to form a handle.

**7** Tie a bead or button to each end.

*I have two older sisters!*

**8** Paint your shield with the face of Medusa and her hair of snakes. See who is brave enough to look at her.

# HOW TO EAT AND DRINK LIKE THE GODS

After a hard day's battling, the great gods on Mount Olympus needed a little refreshment. They didn't eat ordinary food as mortal people did. They had ambrosia and nectar. It was thought that if a mortal ate it, they would become a god!

# AMBROSIA

 **1** First, wash your hands.

 **2** Make the jelly according to the instructions on the packet.

 **3** Add the honey, stirring well.

**4** In the large bowl, whisk the cream until it stands in soft peaks.

**5** Slowly fold the jelly into the cream.

**6** Pour into the dishes and leave to set.

# NECTAR

 **1** Put all the ingredients into the blender and blend for 10 seconds.

 **2** Pour into the glasses.

# HOW TO DECORATE YOUR DRINK

The Ancient Greeks would think it strange to throw away containers as we do today. They decorated their drinking cups and vases with exciting stories from the myths. Many of them have beautiful shapes. Use your stencils to transform some modern containers into Ancient Greek works of art.

## YOU'LL NEED:
Clean plastic containers with tops, drinks cans, sandpaper, stencils, pencil, acrylic paints and brushes, flour and varnish (optional).

## TOP TIP - TOP TIP
Keep the container tops. They are handy to hold on to when painting.

**1**   Roughen the surface of your containers or drinks cans with the sandpaper. This will help the paint to stick.

**2**   Hold your container by its top or with a pencil in the top of a can. Paint with white acrylic paint.

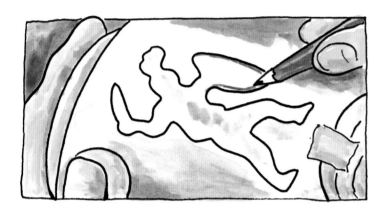

**3**   Hold your stencil in place and draw the outline in pencil. (A friend could help to hold it steady for you.)

**4**   Paint in the shapes and build them out by adding a bit of flour to the paint to thicken it.

**5**   Leave to dry well before adding more thick paint.

**6**   You can varnish it to keep the colours bright. Make sure the paint is completely dry first.

# HOW TO WRITE ANCIENT GREEK

The Ancient Greeks invented the first alphabet in the world that had signs for vowels and consonants. The word 'alphabet' is made from the names of its first two letters. Use the signs to write your name or as a secret code with a friend. If you visit Greece, you will be able to read the shop signs. There have been changes to the pronunciation, but the letters are the same as they were nearly 3,000 years ago!

| Greek Letter | Name | Sound | Greek Letter | Name | Sound |
|---|---|---|---|---|---|
| A α | alpha | J<u>a</u>ck | H η | eta | s<u>ee</u> |
| B β | beta | <u>B</u>illy | Θ θ | theta | Be<u>th</u> |
| Γ γ | gamma | <u>G</u>race | I ι | iota | K<u>i</u>t |
| Δ δ | delta | <u>D</u>aisy | K κ | kappa | Ni<u>ck</u>y |
| E ε | epsilon | <u>E</u>mily | Λ λ | lambda | Ji<u>ll</u> |
| Z ζ | zeta | <u>Z</u>oë | M μ | mu | <u>m</u>at |

| Greek Letter | Name | Sound | Greek Letter | Name | Sound |
|---|---|---|---|---|---|
| N ν | nu | <u>N</u>oddy | Τ τ | tau | s<u>t</u>op |
| Ξ ξ | xi | ki<u>ck</u>s | Υ υ | upsilon | <u>U</u>na |
| Ο ο | omicron | B<u>o</u>b | Φ φ | phi | <u>Ph</u>il |
| Π π | pi | <u>p</u>ony | Χ χ | chi | <u>Kh</u>an |
| Ρ ρ | rho | <u>R</u>ory | Ψ ψ | psi | li<u>ps</u> |
| Σ σ ς | sigma | <u>S</u>arah | Ω ω | omega | R<u>o</u>wan |

**TELEPHONE**
WE'VE MADE NEW WORDS FROM ANCIENT GREEK ONES. 'TELE' MEANS 'FAR' AND 'PHONE' MEANS 'SOUND'. SEE IF YOU CAN FIND ANY MORE.

I'll see you later.

# ANCIENT GREECE

Four thousand years ago, Europe's first civilizations began on the island of Crete and around the city of Mycenae. They were destroyed by earthquakes and war, but new cities took their place. The most powerful of these were Athens and Sparta.

**2,600–1,400 BC**
The first European civilization, called Minoan, began on the island of Crete.

**1,400–1,100 BC**
The Golden Age of Mycenae.

**1,200 BC**
Troy was besieged and destroyed by the Greeks.

# THE GREEK MYTHS

The most famous Greek myth is the story of the warrior king, Odysseus, and his return home from Troy. The voyage took ten years. All his men were eaten by giants or killed by sea-monsters. Alone and dressed as a beggar, Odysseus defeated the last of his enemies and reclaimed his kingdom. Today the word 'odyssey' means a long journey full of adventures.

**1,200-900 BC**
Mycenae was destroyed in an age of war and destruction.

**750 BC**
Homer composed the epic story-poems, the *Iliad* and the *Odyssey*.

**480-336 BC**
Athens became powerful. This was the Classical Age.

# HOW TO DRAW YOURSELF AS AN ANCIENT GREEK

Ancient Greek art is famous for its quality and beauty. The Greeks knew that their buildings and statues looked better when their design followed a rule called the golden mean. This was a rectangle drawn at a ratio of 1 to 1.618 and based on the measurements and shape of the human body.

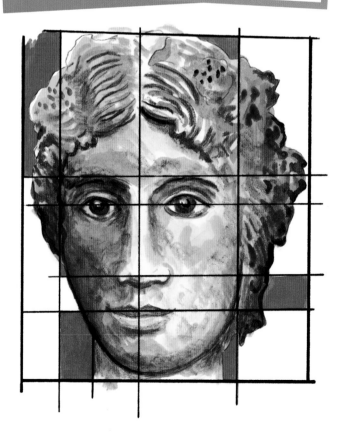

## YOU'LL NEED:
Pencil, paper, ruler, mirror, pencil rubber, paints or crayons.

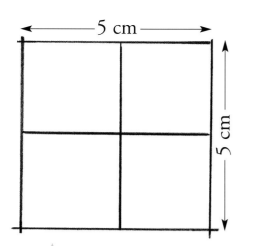

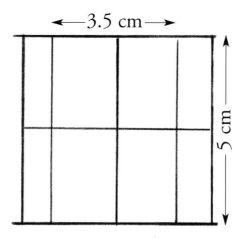

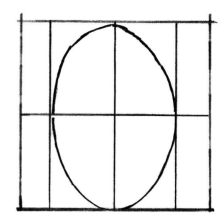

1 Draw a square 5 x 5 cm. Divide it into 4 equal parts.

2 Draw 2 lines to form a rectangle 5 x 3.5 cm. Draw an oval shape inside it.

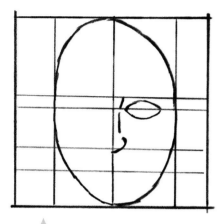

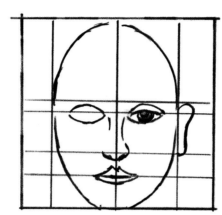

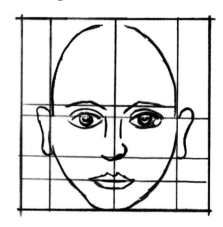

3 Look in the mirror and begin drawing your face as shown.

4 The tip of the nose is halfway between the eyes and chin. The mouth is halfway between the nose and chin.

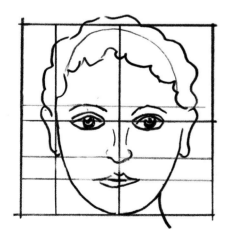

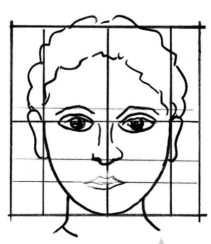

5 Rub out the guide lines and finish off with paints or crayons.

**15**

# HOW TO MAKE THE HELMET OF HADES

This helmet belonged to Hades, the god of the underworld. Whoever wore it became invisible, so it was very handy for fighting monsters and giants. All the Ancient Greek heroes wanted a go with it. In the myths, Hades lent it to Perseus to help him kill the gorgon, Medusa.

## TOP TIP – TOP TIP
Use a marker pen to draw in details around the eyes and mouth.

## YOU'LL NEED:
2 x 2-litre plastic bottles, sandpaper, scissors, thin card, pencil, tracing paper, masking tape, ruler, marker pen, double-sided tape, acrylic paint and brushes.

If you do it right, when you put it on you should look like this:

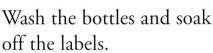

**1** Wash the bottles and soak off the labels.

**2** Roughen the bottles' surfaces with sandpaper.

5 cm

Back view

Side view

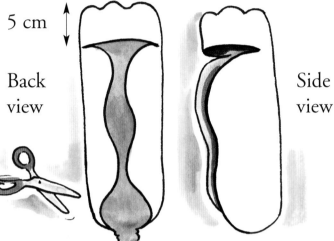

**3** Cut out as shown. Take care.

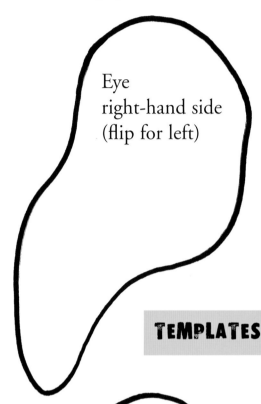

Eye
right-hand side
(flip for left)

**TEMPLATES**

Mouth

14 cm from top

Front view

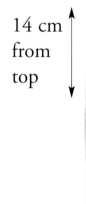

**4** Copy the templates on to thin card. (See how to on the inside front cover.) Use them as a guide to draw and cut out the eyes and mouth openings.

**5** Cut a strip from the other bottle to use as a headband. Adjust to fit and stick with double-sided tape. Paint the helmet.

**17**

# HOW TO MAKE PANDORA'S BOX

Pandora was the first woman. She was made from clay by the god Hephaestos in the shape of the beautiful goddess, Aphrodite. Zeus gave her a closed box and said it must never be opened. She really tried hard not to look inside, but just had to take a peep. Out flew every evil thing in the world. The only thing left was hope, stuck to the lid and fluttering like a tiny butterfly.

### YOU'LL NEED:
Card (from a cereal box), thin paper, 15-cm elastic hair band, C6 size envelope, double-sided tape, scissors, pencil, craft knife, ruler, paints, brushes and felt-tips.

DO NOT OPEN!

**1** Cut a piece of card 14 x 7 cm. Draw and score 4 lines and cut 4 small notches as shown.

**2** Fold as shown.

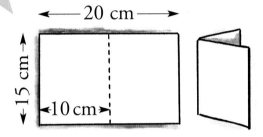

20 cm
15 cm
10 cm

**3** Cut another piece of card 20 x 15 cm. Fold it in half and decorate the front.

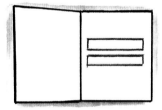

**4** Draw 2 rectangles (7 x 2 cm) on the card, 5 cm from the top and 0.5 cm apart.

flattens this way

**6** Stretch the elastic hair band around the notches. Make a small 'hope' and stick it to the top. Cut some small nasties from thin paper and place on top. Press and hold flat.

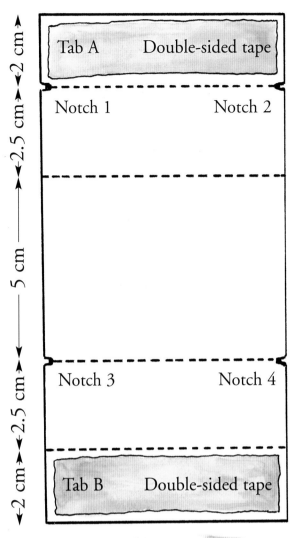

2 cm
2.5 cm
5 cm
2.5 cm
2 cm

Tab A        Double-sided tape

Notch 1        Notch 2

Notch 3        Notch 4

Tab B        Double-sided tape

**5** Carefully stick tabs A and B to the rectangles with double-sided tape.

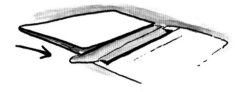

**7** Carefully close the card and place in the envelope, open side first. When opened the little nasties will be flung out.

**19**

# HOW TO MAKE A WINNER'S OLIVE WREATH

The first Olympic Games were held in Greece nearly 2,800 years ago. The winners were given a wreath to wear, made from olive leaves. The Ancient Greeks stopped all fighting while the games were on. An olive branch is still the symbol of peace today.

## YOU'LL NEED:

Thick green paper at least 63 cm wide, a small piece of card, tracing paper, masking tape, scissors, ruler, pencil, glue, paints and brushes and/or metallic pens.

## TOP TIP – TOP TIP

Make more leaves by cutting through several layers of paper at once.

20

63 cm

5 cm

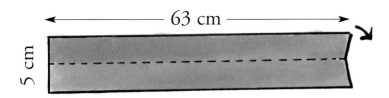

**1** Cut a piece of paper 5 x 63 cm and fold it in half.

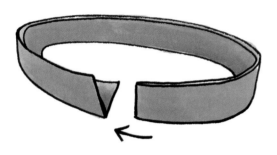

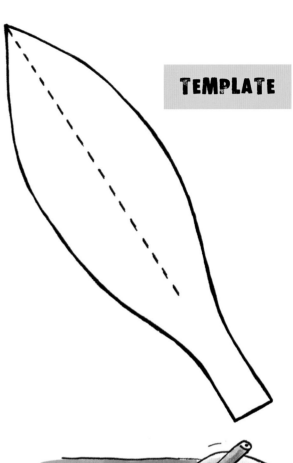

**2** Slide one end into the other until it fits your head and glue.

**3** Copy the template on to the card (see the instructions on the inside front cover) and cut it out.

**4** Draw round the shape on the green paper and cut it out to make a leaf. Make lots more.

**5** Fold the leaves in half. Glue the stalks into the headband. Don't make them look too neat.

**6** You can paint them if you like and let them dry. Some wreaths were made of gold or silver.

# SYMBOLS FROM THE MYTHS

All great stories need a great set of characters. The Greek myths had a fabulous line-up. Have a look at some of the myths, then try making up your own stories using some of these symbols.

Helmet

Sword

Helmets and swords often had magical powers.

Shield

The goddess Athene gave Perseus a shield polished like a mirror. He looked at the gorgon, Medusa, through it and that stopped him being turned to stone.

Arrow

Eros, the cheeky little god of love, shot people with gold-tipped arrows and they fell in love.

Jason and the Argonauts sailed to the very edge of the world in search of the Golden Fleece.

Dolphin

Dolphins guided ships and took messages for the gods.

Pegasus, the flying horse. A useful friend in an emergency.

Beautiful Princess

Princess Ariadne helped Theseus escape from the labyrinth after he killed the Minotaur.

Thunderbolt of Zeus

Doric Column

Ionic Column

Corinthian Column

Scary Monster

One of the best known monsters was the Minotaur. He had the head of a bull and the body of a man – the first cowboy perhaps?

Vases were painted with scenes from the myths.

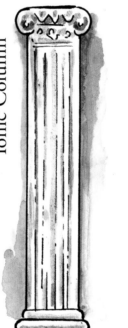

Brave Warrior

He was always ready to fight monsters and giants.

**23**

# HOW TO USE YOUR STENCILS

Cut or tear off the stencil sheet from the back of the book. Choose a shape and place it over your paper. Hold it there with masking tape. Draw the outline with soft pencil. Use pages 22-23 as a guide to colouring and giving detail to your shapes.

## TOP TIP – TOP TIP
Keep stencils as clean as possible. Wipe off surplus paint. Let paint dry between stencilling.

## TOOTHBRUSH SPRAY

**1** Mask off the other stencils. Dip an old toothbrush in paint. Hold it about 5 cm above the stencil. Flick the paint off the brush with a strip cut from a plastic container.

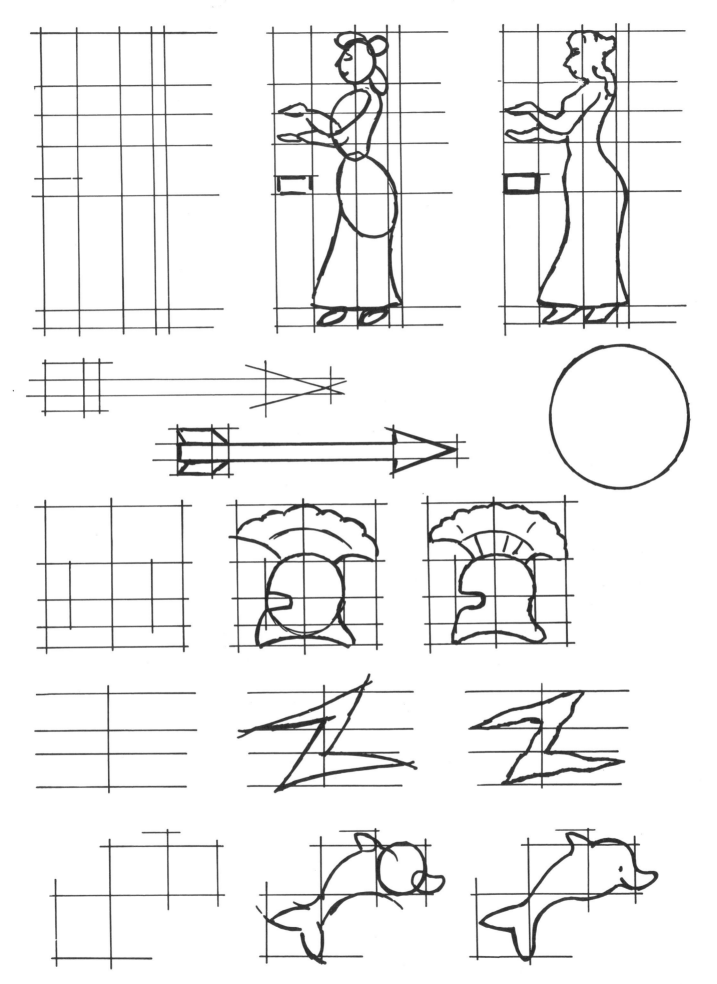

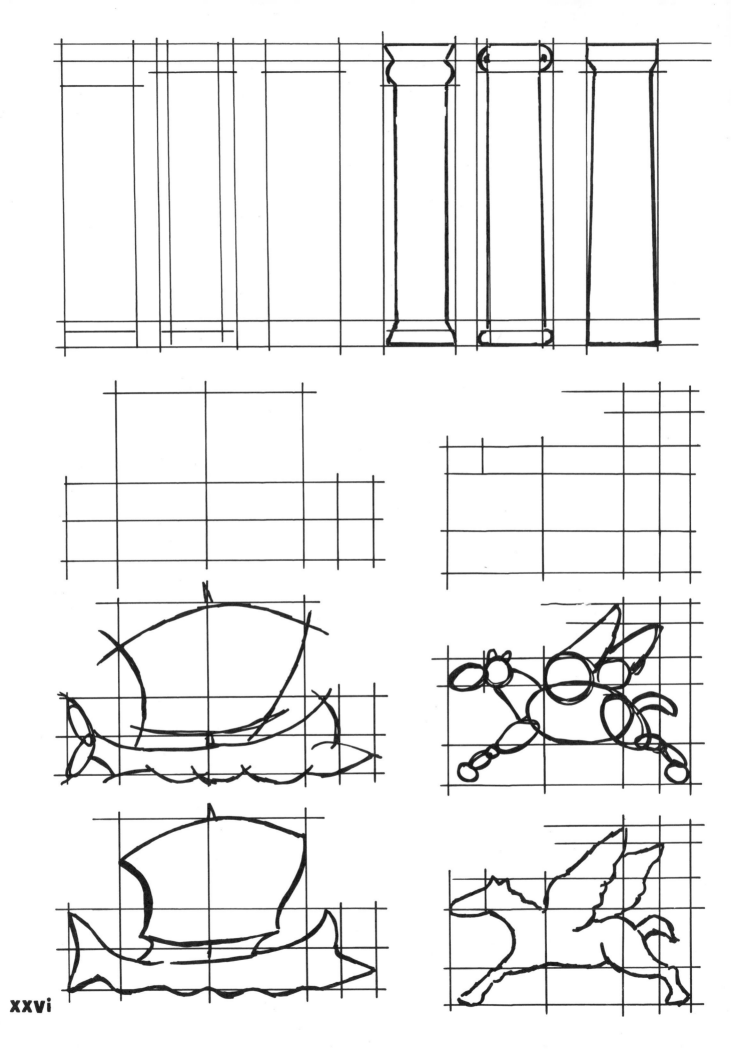